C000120099

NOTTINGHAM

LIFE IN THE POSTWAR YEARS

DOUGLAS WHITWORTH

SUTTON PUBLISHING

Sutton Publishing Limited
Phoenix Mill · Thrupp · Stroud
Gloucestershire · GL5 2BU

First published 2006

Title page photograph: Drury Hill in 1946 –
Nottingham's most photogenic and
lamented street. *(FWS)*

British Library Cataloguing in Publication Data
A catalogue record for this book is available from the
British Library.

ISBN 0-7509-4367-X

Typeset in 10.5/13.5 Photina.
Typesetting and origination by
Sutton Publishing Limited.
Printed and bound in England by
J.H. Haynes & Co. Ltd, Sparkford.

The Council House from the air, showing the huddle of small properties surrounding the great
building, 1950. *(NEP)*

CONTENTS

Theatre Square from Wollaton Street on a showery morning with the sun's rays lighting up the façades of the County Hotel and the Theatre Royal, 1950s. *(FWS)*

INTRODUCTION

In common with other major cities Nottingham has changed considerably since the end of the Second World War, and even now plans are being made to alter the face of the city again.

Nottingham was more fortunate than many other provincial cities as it did not suffer too heavily from German bombing and the city council had no need to plan and rebuild with any urgency. The slum clearance programme which was halted in 1939 was not recommenced until 1945 – the year in which land for council house building was acquired in Clifton. To help meet the demand for accommodation over 1,000 prefabricated houses were built in Beechdale and Aspley in the first two postwar years; some of these are still in use.

Postwar Nottingham was a prosperous city with a variety of trades, although the traditional lace industry was in decline. The city's three major companies – Boots, Raleigh and Players – were recovering from wartime restrictions and enjoying a growing prosperity.

Boots was still basically a pharmaceutical and toiletries concern with a retail shop in almost every high street in the country. Raleigh Cycles were world-famous, and as the age of the car for almost every family had not yet arrived, the home market was very strong. Players had not yet diversified, but the market for cigarettes was enormous and to work at Players seemed to be the ultimate achievement for Nottingham people.

Ericsson Telephones, now Siemens Communications, situated just outside the city, employed many hundreds of Nottingham people, as did British Rail. In addition to these major employers, there were hundreds of smaller companies, all contributing towards making Nottingham a thriving city.

The harsh winter of 1946–7 was, however, a setback to the recovery of Nottingham's businesses. Freezing temperatures and heavy snow which lasted for several weeks caused major power cuts to industry. The floods which followed reached the highest level of the century and inundated the Meadows and other low-lying areas of the city. The huge damage which the rising waters caused prompted the authorities to act to prevent such floods occurring again and a flood defence scheme was introduced.

In 1949 the citizens of Nottingham who, like the remainder of the British people, were undergoing greater hardships and restrictions than during the Second World War, were given the opportunity to celebrate. The occasion was the 500th anniversary of the granting of the Great Charter to the borough, significantly increasing its powers and privileges. The celebrations included a royal visit by Princess Elizabeth and the Duke of Edinburgh, exhibitions, pageants, sporting events and a Nottingham Symphony composed by Alan Bush.

Four years later Nottingham, like other towns and cities, celebrated the Coronation of Queen Elizabeth II with parades and pageants, but those with long memories will remember it as the first major event they witnessed on television – probably in a neighbour's house – on a 9-inch screen.

Live theatre was very popular: the Playhouse on Goldsmith Street, although run on a shoestring, was producing a consistently high level of entertainment. It was not until 1963, after great controversy, that the new Playhouse in East Circus Street was opened. The Theatre Royal was at the same time showing a variety of plays, pantomime, ballet and opera. Great actors such as John Gielgud, Laurence Olivier and Donald Wolfit could be seen here; at fifteen years of age Julie Andrews appeared in the 1950–1 pantomime. The Empire Theatre was giving twice-nightly variety shows with some of the great comedians of the day. The challenge from television was then small but with falling attendances the theatre was closed in 1958.

Sport in the years following the Second World War was eagerly followed. This was the time when the legendary Tommy Lawton played for Notts County – he drew huge crowds to Meadow Lane and high-scoring matches were frequent. Nottingham Forest, under Billy Walker's management, were promoted to the First Division in 1957 and won the FA Cup two years later in a classic game of football. At Trent Bridge, while the county cricket team never won any championships, some of the great players of the time appeared there in test matches. Don Bradman came in 1948 along with Keith Miller, Ray Lindwall, Lindsey Hassett and others. The Nottingham Panthers ice hockey team, formed in 1946, attracted enthusiastic crowds to the Ice Stadium to watch the exciting games played there. The star player of that era was Chick Zamick, a high-scoring forward.

By the 1950s the ownership of private cars became more commonplace and in consequence traffic jams around the city centre were frequent. To alleviate the congestion on the city's roads, work on the construction of Maid Marian Way began in the late 1950s. This involved the destruction of many fine buildings, notably the Collin's Almshouses on Friary Lane.

Another contentious project was the construction of the Broad Marsh Shopping Centre which involved the destruction of Drury Hill, the ancient road south out of Nottingham. Despite great opposition, this much-loved street was submerged in the new building. The construction of the Victoria Shopping Centre to the north of the city centre also caused considerable controversy. The Victoria Railway Station, which was demolished in 1967 to make way for the centre, was a victim of Dr Beeching's rationalisation of Britain's railways.

The two new precincts changed the shopping habits of Nottingham people and some larger stores in the city centre either moved into one of them or eventually closed down.

The 1960s was also the decade when several distinctive buildings were demolished to be replaced by bland concrete blocks – these included Lloyds Bank on Beastmarket Hill, the Oriental Café in Wheeler Gate and, most lamented of all, the Black Boy Hotel on Long Row.

Plans were drawn up in the 1960s for the clearance of slum properties in St Ann's, the Meadows, Hyson Green and Basford, all of which had strong social identities. The redevelopment of the districts began in the early 1970s, with St Ann's being almost entirely cleared – despite determined opposition. In Basford and Hyson Green, high-rise flats were constructed which were to perpetuate the squalor of the houses they had replaced.

The thirty years following the end of the Second World War covered by this personal view of Nottingham were a great opportunity for the city council to plan and build a better city. That opportunity was largely missed but the civic authorities are now more aware of Nottingham's heritage, and are hopefully following a policy of conserving the best of the past without sacrificing the future.

1

The Old Market Square

Vehicle headlights making ribbons of light down Market Street and across the Old Market Square, 1965. The department stores of Griffin & Spalding and Pearson Bros on Long Row were major attractions to the shoppers of Nottingham – the two city shopping centres were then still at an early planning stage. *(NEP)*

The imposing Council House dwarfing the surrounding buildings, 1952. The citizens of Nottingham had by then become accustomed to Slab Square where they could sit in the sunshine, in a calm space away from the bustle of traffic. The white marble statue of Queen Victoria still dominated the western end of the square, but in 1953 it was removed to the Memorial Gardens on the Victoria Embankment. *(JM)*

Opposite, top: The portico of the Council House, with a visitor in discussion with the long-coated commissionaire, 1948. The original plans of Cecil Howitt envisaged the internal shopping arcade extending to the front of the building but the city council argued that this would not be dignified. The architect's revised design of a portico and grand entrance leading to a sweeping staircase was accepted and the Council House was officially opened by the Prince of Wales on 22 May 1929. *(FWS)*

Opposite, bottom: The dome of the Council House rising above the rooftops of Nottingham, 1954. From a distance the dome seems too high, but this was deliberate to allow it to be seen from the base of the building. In the foreground are two of Watson Fothergill's buildings: on the left, the tower of the Westminster Bank on Thurland Street, and in the centre, the conical tower of the Express Buildings on Upper Parliament Street. *(FWS)*

Crowds line Long Row for the arrival of Princess Elizabeth and the Duke of Edinburgh during the Quincentenary week in 1949. The celebrations were held to commemorate the 500th anniversary of the granting of the Great Charter to Nottingham by Henry VI. This royal charter gave the town the status of a county in its own right and the privilege of self-government. The events included exhibitions, sports, a medieval fair, fireworks and numerous concerts including the première of the Nottingham Symphony by Alan Bush. *(FWS)*

Robin Hood was an obvious figurehead for this socialist parade on Long Row during the Quincentenary week. The biggest event of the celebrations was an historical pageant held at the Ice Stadium which depicted a cavalcade of scenes from Nottingham's history. *(JDW)*

The Carlton cinema in Chapel Bar decorated for the Quincentenary. The whole city became involved in the celebrations which were a great boost to everyone's morale, coming at a time of great stringency. The Carlton opened in October 1939, showing *Jamaica Inn* starring Charles Laughton and Maureen O'Hara. After several name changes and a conversion to a triple-screen cinema, the ABC, as it was finally known, closed in 1999. *(JDW)*

Queen Elizabeth II arrives for a civic reception in the Council House, 1955. Behind the mace bearer on the right is the Lord Mayor, Councillor Leonard Mitson, and on the left is the Lord Lieutenant of the County, the Duke of Portland. The Queen and the Duke of Edinburgh spent the day in Nottingham watching a dance display by schoolchildren on the Forest, visiting Birkin's lace factory and attending the Royal Show in Wollaton Park. *(NEP)*

Opposite: The Council House and the Old Market Square floodlit for the Coronation of Queen Elizabeth II in 1953. Towns and cities throughout the country vied with each other to present the best display of flags and banners. The Coronation was the first great television event, with large numbers of people huddled round small television screens to watch the dawn of a new era. Britons truly believed that the dreary days of austerity were behind them and that a new Elizabethan age was beginning. *(NEP)*

The Black Boy Hotel, seen here in 1953, with its fantastic frontage, was the centrepiece of this stretch of Long Row. Watson Fothergill extended the hotel in 1878 and nine years later rebuilt the façade, retaining the fashionable colonnade. For three-quarters of a century the hotel played host to many famous people and was also a favourite of the local population. Although protests were voiced at the prospect of the Black Boy closing, the hotel shut its doors for the last time on 8 March 1969, to be replaced by a utilitarian Littlewoods store. *(VI)*

Skinner & Rook, Long Row, 1953. The business was opened by Mr Skinner in 1844; he was joined by Mr Rook in 1860. They quickly built up a reputation for superior produce and fine wines, allied to first-class service. In 1955 the Long Row shop was closed but the company retained a wine and spirits store in Maypole Yard. *(VI)*

Three of the numerous shoe shops on Long Row in the 1950s. Women were then spoilt for choice when shopping for shoes along this parade. These elegant buildings fortunately still survive, spared when the adjoining Black Boy Hotel was demolished. *(VI)*

Opposite, top: The Flying Horse Hotel, The Poultry, 1973. This hotel, which was saved from demolition in 1968, became part of the Chef & Brewer chain and for another twenty years continued to be a popular rendezvous for the citizens of Nottingham. Over the years the hotel has had numerous facelifts but in 1987 the property was gutted and converted into a shopping arcade. *(LB)*

Opposite, bottom: St James's Street, one of the narrowest thoroughfares in Nottingham, 1964. Its old-fashioned charm was spoilt by the construction of Maid Marian Way which bisected the street and by the modern tower blocks which are completely out of character. *(JDW)*

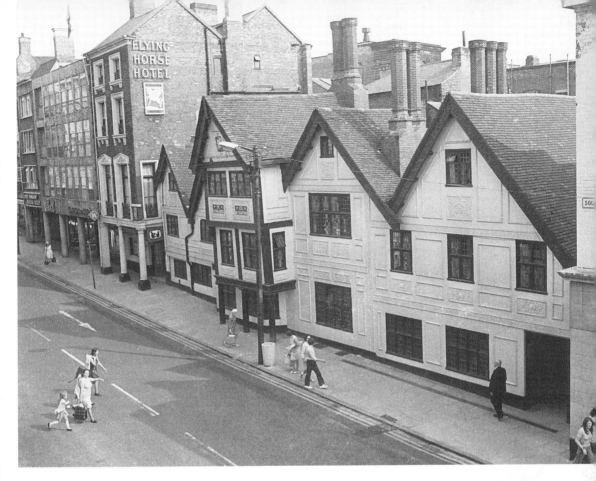

Elizabeth King's pork-pie shop on Beastmarket Hill in 1953, a hundred years after it was established. The premises of Leek & Moorlands Building Society are where John Player opened his first shop in Nottingham. Arriving in the town in 1862 from Saffron Walden he began business as an agent for manures and seeds. His sideline of selling tobacco in 'screws' took over and in 1877 he began manufacturing ready-rolled cigarettes in a small factory in Broad Marsh. These buildings were pulled down in 1966 prior to the construction of the Market Square House. *(VI)*

Beastmarket Hill in 1952, with the buildings sporting a variety of advertising signs, including the famous Guinness clock. Fifty Shilling Tailors were shortly to change their name: suits were advertised in the windows for £6 19s 6d. King's Restaurant was in the basement, and well-patronised – in the morning by businessmen for coffee, and later by shoppers, either for lunch or afternoon tea. A branch of Barclays Bank was to replace these buildings in the early 1960s. *(VI)*

The Oriental Café, Wheeler Gate. 1944. This café, owned by Armitage Bros, was noted for the freshly ground coffee it served to customers in alcoves on the first floor. This seventeenth-century building was also famous for its magnificent plaster ceiling which was saved when the building was demolished in 1960. Although originally intended for Newdigate House, the plasterwork ceiling was first removed to Holme Pierrepont Hall and in 1998 to a house in Ladbroke Square, London. *(LSL)*

Wheeler Gate in 1952 with a row of well-known shops of the time. A. & P. Lake were old-established butchers, the Nottingham Rubber Co. was the shop for raincoats, and beyond were the Scotch Wool Store, the Meadow grocery shop and Boots Day and Night branch. The building above the archway which leads to Eldon Chambers is one of the many elegant Georgian houses which once graced the streets of Nottingham. *(VI)*

A Sunday newspaper vendor in the Old Market Square, 1954. The international crisis of that time was the Chinese threat to Formosa, now Taiwan, but the *Sunday Pictorial* placard declares 'Rubirosa tells all' – this referred to Porfirio Rubirosa, a playboy whose women friends included Zsa Zsa Gabor and Barbara Hutton, the Woolworth heiress. *(picturethepast.org.uk)*

The demolition of the Information Bureau at the bottom of St James's Street in 1946. This was a temporary building for the duration of the war. Queen Victoria on her pedestal is unperturbed, but has only another seven years before being removed herself – to the Victoria Embankment Gardens. *(JDW)*

An anti-aircraft gun on display in the Old Market Square, 1948. The young children appear to be in full control of the weapon. *(JDW)*

2

The Inner City

Market Street in 1953, with a sign on the left directing traffic through the Old Market Square to the Nottingham Aerodrome at Tollerton. The splendid Victorian buildings on the left were still occupied by businesses founded in that era, although both Kent & Cooper Ltd and G.W. Darby were to close within fifteen years. *(VI)*

The city centre from the air in 1953, when the only tall buildings are the Council House and three inner-city churches. The Old Market Square is the only open space in the densely packed streets and yards of the centre of Nottingham. *(NEP)*

Opposite, top: Upper Parliament Street from Park Row, 1966. Maid Marian Way was being extended to this junction and after the demolition of these buildings a traffic roundabout and an underpass were built. The city council planned an expressway around the city centre, but the controversy aroused by the construction of Maid Marian Way resulted in the abandonment of the project. In the background is the Nottingham Co-operative store which was then an attraction to all Co-op members, who received a dividend on every purchase. *(NEP)*

Opposite, bottom: The County Hotel (adjoining the Theatre Royal), The Quadrant, 1971. The County started life as the Clarendon in 1869, changing its name to the Rufford and finally becoming the County in 1923. Over the years many of the performers at the Theatre Royal and the Empire Theatre stayed at the hotel, and the bars were also convenient for patrons of the theatres. Although the Department of the Environment was urged to list the County as a protected building, the hotel, which was the nearest Nottingham had to a Regency crescent, was demolished in 1975. *(AA)*

Above: Victorian buildings at the top of Market Street in 1952. Kent & Cooper Ltd were the best-known piano dealers in the city and also hired out rooms to piano teachers and examiners. The business was to close in 1968. G.W. Darby's glass and china shop was equally well regarded and noted for its high-class wares. Beyond Darby's is the Constitutional Club, founded in 1832 and opened in Market Street in 1899. After its closure in 1959 the building was sold to the Borough Club which occupied it for only ten years before it became a Berni Inn with the emotive name the Black Boy. *(VI)*

Market Street with the Scala cinema on the extreme right, 1952. The building was opened in 1875 as the Alexandra Skating Rink and within a year was converted into the Talbot Palace of Varieties. After a number of further name changes it became the Scala cinema in 1913, retaining this title until 1964, after which the cinema went through several reincarnations until it became the Robin Hood Tavern, which finally closed in 1988. *(VI)*

The Guardian office decorated for the Coronation of Queen Elizabeth II in 1953. Until the closure of the *Evening Post*'s sister paper, the *Nottingham Guardian* in 1973, this was the name of the building at the corner of South Sherwood Street and Forman Street. Thomas Forman bought a publishing business on Long Row in 1849 which printed the *Nottinghamshire Guardian*, and after building this corner block in 1871–2 he launched the *Evening Post* in 1878. Publication of the *Post* continued here until 1998 when the editorial offices moved to Castle Wharf House, with the paper being printed in Derby. *(NEP)*

The demolition of the Mechanics Institute and Cinema in 1964, giving a new view of the Victoria Railway Station. After the clearance of the site Birkbeck House was built, which itself was pulled down in 2005 for a new development. *(JDW)*

The Trinity Square car park, 1965. This had only recently been opened, controversially replacing Holy Trinity Church. This typical 1960s block is now being replaced with, hopefully, a more attractive structure. On the left is the Victoria Hotel, originally the railway hotel and now given a facelift as the Nottingham Hilton. *(JDW)*

Marsden's Café and the New Milton Restaurant, Milton Street, 1952. These art deco buildings were built in 1929 replacing older ones similar to those on the right. They were both popular establishments but were closed in the 1960s. *(VI)*

The Milton's Head Hotel at the corner of Milton Street and Lower Parliament Street in 1969, shortly after its closure. In the 1960s the downstairs bar was the venue for aspiring guitarists and blues singers. *(AA)*

Milton Street from the roof of Birkbeck House, 1965. On the left is the Welbeck Hotel with its multiple chimneys, and in its last decade. In the 1960s Nottingham's traffic problems were becoming increasingly difficult and a zone and collar system to restrict vehicles from the city centre was introduced; it was abandoned as a failure. Luxurious Lilac Leopard coaches were brought into use to provide park-and-ride services for car drivers but these did not achieve their aim and were discontinued. The council is still struggling with the problem of inner-city traffic and has reintroduced many of the schemes already attempted. *(NEP)*

The clock tower of the Victoria Station dwarfed by the Victoria Centre flats, 1973. The tower is all that remains of the station, which is still mourned by many Nottingham people. The station building was a monument to the great era of railway travel and was superbly constructed. A proposal that the railway line and station should be incorporated into the new shopping centre went unheeded, and Nottingham lost its only north–south railway line. (JDW)

The Old Corner Pin, Upper Parliament Street, 1955. This eighteenth-century inn began life as the George and by 1799 had become the Horse and Groom, before taking its later title in 1910. After its closure in 1989 the Old Corner Pin was converted into a Disney store and is now a branch of Miss Selfridge. *(FWS)*

Cars line both sides of Lower Parliament Street, 1964. On the right is the art deco Market Garage and on the extreme left is the Admiral Duncan from the same period. *(VI)*

The Bodega, Pelham Street, 1950s. This distinctive public house was built in 1902 on the site of the Durham Ox, then in a dilapidated state. The Bodega was noted for its port and sherry and also had a billiard room on its upper floor. After a number of name changes in the recent past the pub is now called the Social. *(VI)*

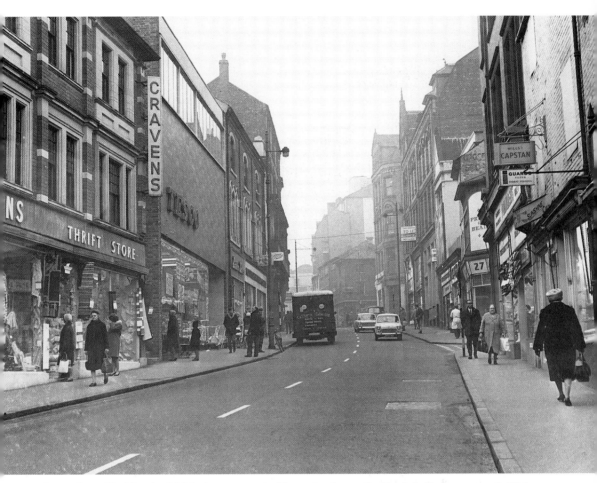

Goose Gate, Hockley, in 1964, then a street of bargain shops. On the left, Cravens were built in 1933 on the site of Jesse Boot's first shop. Higher up the street, Boots were still trading in Jesse's first purpose-built shop, opened in 1883. Among the other well-known shops in Hockley at the time were Ashmores, whose arcade was very popular, and several clothiers, including Butler Morris, Harrisons, Prossers and Price & Beal. *(JDW)*

Opposite, top: A group of interesting buildings on Carlton Street, 1952. J. & H. Bell Ltd on the right was one of the oldest companies in Nottingham, having been founded in 1800. Besides being booksellers and printers, Bell's also had a private circulating library. The unusual building next to Bell's began life as the bank of J. & J.C. Wright, which in 1898 merged with the Capital & Counties Bank. This bank in turn was taken over in 1918 by Lloyds, and was to remain open until 1995. These two buildings have been transformed – Bell's until recently into Sonny's Restaurant and Lloyds Bank into Lloyds No. 1 Coffee Bar. *(VI)*

Opposite, bottom: A traffic warden at the corner of George Street and Carlton Street, 1964. This was the year in which traffic wardens were first introduced onto the city's streets in an endeavour to reduce illegal parking by motorists. In the background are two old-established Nottingham businesses, Finch's the haberdashers and John Lees, famous for its knitting wool. *(JDW)*

Drury Hill, 1964. Sufficient critical words over the destruction of this narrow winding street have been written to fill a book. This was the old road south from Nottingham and was scheduled for demolition when the Broad Marsh Shopping Centre was planned in the late 1960s. Despite objections from local environmental groups, the much-loved street was demolished to be replaced by an escalator. *(JL)*

Vault Hall, Low Pavement, 1950. The house on the corner of Drury Hill was the home, in the eighteenth century, of Abigail Gawthern, the diarist. She lived through momentous times, but she also recorded everyday local occurrences. Nearer the present day, W.A. Sime the barrister, and also from 1947 to 1950 the captain of the Nottinghamshire County Cricket Club, had his chambers in this building. *(VI)*

Severns on Middle Pavement, 1968. John and James Severn began their wine and spirit business in the adjoining Georgian house in 1735, but it was not until 1900 that they acquired the small fifteenth-century timber-framed building. In spite of valiant efforts by conservationists, both houses were pulled down in 1968 before the construction of the Broad Marsh Shopping Centre; the medieval house was, however, re-erected on Castle Road. *(JL)*

Lister Gate, 1950. Four well-known businesses were adjacent on this stretch of the road: Lennon Bros the tobacconists, Dewhursts the butchers, Weavers, wine and spirit merchants, and Boots Cash Chemists. Weavers, besides being retailers, also had a public bar, and in Castle Gate a bar for men only. The business was established in 1844 by Edmund Weaver and purchased by George Trease in 1897. After redevelopment of these buildings in 1960 Alan Trease continued the wine and spirit business in the company's premises in Castle Gate. *(VI)*

Opposite, top: A deserted Lister Gate in 1950, shortly after the removal of the Walter Fountain from this junction. The fountain had been erected in 1866 as a memorial to John Walter, MP for Nottingham and the proprietor of *The Times.* The fountain was sacrificed in a road improvement scheme, being replaced by a mini roundabout. *(VI)*

Opposite, bottom: Lister Gate during the construction of the Broad Marsh Shopping Centre, 1973. The building of Nottingham's second shopping precinct was within a year of completion although the official opening ceremony was not performed until 1975. Thirty years later there are again plans to rebuild the centre, which was never as successful as the Victoria Centre. *(LB)*

Shoppers in Lister Gate on a busy Saturday afternoon in 1975. As well as the recently opened Broad Marsh Centre, several of the city's cash-trade stores were sited in this area: Woolworths, British Home Stores and Marks & Spencer. *(D. Archer)*

The temporary car park behind the Portland Hotel, Carrington Street, 1965. This land between Canal Street and the Nottingham Canal, previously occupied by several factories, was to become the site of the Nottingham Crown Courts. *(JDW)*

3

Around the Castle

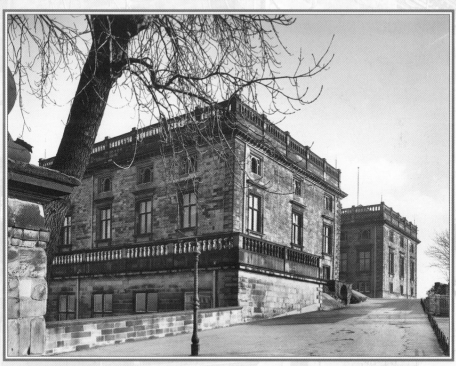

Nottingham Castle, 1951. When T.C. Hine restored the fire-damaged building in 1878, the external staircases on the east front were removed; to compensate for this he built a colonnade and new entrance on the west front. Tourists seeking a traditional castle may be disappointed but the building remains a major baroque palace in all but name. *(VI)*

Castle Road in 1949, before most of these buildings were demolished. Mortimer's House on the extreme left, designed by Watson Fothergill and originally planned as a row of offices and shops, was fortunately saved. Further down Castle Road, Jessamine Cottages, an attractive row of eighteenth-century houses, were pulled down before the construction of the People's College of Further Education. A compensation for the loss of these buildings was the reconstruction here in 1970 of Severns, the medieval building removed from Middle Pavement. *(JL)*

Opposite, top: The view towards the city centre from the castle grounds in 1949, then unspoilt by the multi-storey office blocks which have since been built. During the Second World War the castle and grounds were requisitioned by the military and it was not until 1946 that the public were again allowed access. *(JDW)*

Opposite, bottom: Rooftops between Walnut Tree Lane and Castle Terrace viewed from the castle walls in the 1950s. There is a splendid variety of roof-levels and chimneys which were all destined to disappear before the end of the decade in an indiscriminate clearance of the area. *(FWS)*

The unveiling of the statue of Robin Hood outside the walls of Nottingham Castle, July 1952. In the group from the left are the Sheriff of Nottingham, Councillor John Kenyon, the Duchess of Portland who officially unveiled the statue, Philip Clay, the donor, James Woodford, the sculptor, Mrs J. Woodford and the Lord Mayor, Councillor Leon Willson. Although the legend of Robin Hood is known throughout the world, it was not until this time that the city possessed a statue of its most famous character. Philip Clay, a Nottingham businessman, made an offer at the conclusion of the Quincentenary week in 1949, to donate a statue, but the suggestion by the then Lord Mayor that it should be placed in front of the Council House fortunately went unheeded. The garden in which the statue is situated was designed by Cecil Howitt and also contains four smaller statues of Robin's outlaws. *(NEP)*

The caretaker sweeping the path in Collin's Almshouses, Friar Lane, 1955. The garden of the almshouses was an oasis in the centre of the city, but within a year it was to disappear along with the twenty-four almshouses. Built in 1709, they were endowed by Abel Collin, and were considered to be among the finest in the country. Although only part of the land of the almshouses was needed when Maid Marian Way was built, this graceful building was demolished. *(FWS)*

The Nottingham Corporation Water Offices decorated for the Coronation in 1953. The city's water supply was then mainly derived from the corporation's five pumping stations in the county, with the remainder from reservoirs in the Derwent Valley. These were the accounts offices of the Water Board, and the water engineers and surveyors were also located here. In the yard behind were the stores of pipes and other equipment. *(VI)*

Slum clearance in 1950 affording a good view of the castle and the Trip to Jerusalem. This area of tightly packed houses was the last part of Broad Marsh to be demolished. St Nicholas' Church School with its bell tower was built in 1859, but had not been used as a school since 1912. The People's College of Further Education built on the site, and criticised for its poor architecture, is itself now to be demolished. *(NEP)*

Jessamine Cottages on the left and to the right the houses on Castle Terrace – shuttered and awaiting demolition, 1950. Jessamine Cottages were originally the workhouse for the parish of St Nicholas and dated from 1729. When the workhouse moved to Butt Dyke (later renamed Park Row) in 1815, this building was converted into separate cottages. (*FWS*)

The last remants of Walnut Tree Lane, 1964. A foot path remains but the winding and attractive street leading from Castle Road is in use as a temporary car park. On the left, behind the wall and trees, are the gardens of the eighteenth-century houses on Castle Gate which became the Museum of Costume and Textiles. (*JDW*)

Newdigate House, Castle Gate, in 1966 after its restoration. This is probably the most famous house in the city, being the residence of Marshal Tallard from 1705 until 1711, following his capture at the Battle of Blenheim. The Marshal was nominally a prisoner, but was allowed into the town and to visit local dignitaries. Tallard had a garden laid out by Henry Wise, the leading nurseryman of the day, who designed the gardens of Longleat and Blenheim. By 1960 the house was in a neglected state and the city council planned to convert it into a museum, but financial restrictions prevented this. The house was then acquired by the United Services Club as their new home, and recently the ground floor has been opened as the World Service Restaurant. *(JDW)*

Opposite, top: Temporary parking for cars near Maid Marian Way in 1966. The road which had cut through the ancient streets leading to the castle was now being widened and extended to Chapel Bar. After the demolition of the buildings on the west side of the road, the vacant land became a convenient free car park for dozens of cars. *(JDW)*

Opposite, bottom: Newdigate House overwhelmed by a new office block being constructed on Maid Marian Way, 1965. This seventeenth-century house was spared but the adjoining house in the Dutch style was demolished. *(JDW)*

Friar Lane from the roof of the Pearl Assurance building, 1969. The pedestrian underpass built at the junction with Maid Marian Way was quickly seen as a mistake, creating a barrier between the Old Market Square and the castle. Plans were proposed for the dual carriageway to be sunk into a tunnel, but the cost of this was prohibitive and in 2003 work began on filling in the underpass and creating surface crossings. At the same time trees were planted on Maid Marian Way in an attempt to soften the outline of the road. (*JDW*)

Opposite: The Maid Marian Way underpass being constructed in 1965. The civic authority's major concern then was to redirect traffic away from the city centre with little thought as to the impact a dual carriageway would have on an historic area of Nottingham. The buildings which were then constructed on either side of the new road were poorly designed and with no overall plan. (*NEP*)

Castle Gate, 1953. The house on the left is a seventeenth-century structure which was demolished in the 1960s when St Nicholas' Street was widened. The narrow adjoining building was also pulled down with the loss of the stone pillars on each side of the door – and believed to be from the twelfth-century Lenton Priory. *(JDW)*

4

Industry

Princess Elizabeth visits the Trades Exhibition in Broad Marsh during the Quincentenary celebrations in 1949. On the right is the chairman of the exhibition committee, Mr J.G. McMeeking. The four major local firms, Players, Boots, Raleigh and Ericsson were well represented – Players' stand was only a few yards away from the old building where John Player began manufacturing cigarettes on a large scale. *(VI)*

Players' tobacco factories from the air, 1951. The No. 1 Factory, nearest the camera, was built by John Player in 1884 as a speculation. Unwanted space in the factory was rented out to lace-makers. Behind is the striking No. 2 Factory which was designed by Players' own architects and opened in 1932. Production gradually ceased in these factories in the 1970s, with manufacturing being transferred to the new Horizon Factory at Lenton. These factories have now been demolished, the loss of the distinctive No. 2 Factory being the greatest. *(VI)*

Opposite, top: Tobacco being weighed at Players, 1950. After being weighed the leaf is blended and allowed to mature before being fed into cutting machines. The cut tobacco is then introduced into the cigarette-making machines, an automatic process which transfers a controlled amount of tobacco to a cigarette paper before sealing. *(VI)*

Opposite, bottom: Players' 'Angels' operating machines which automatically pack the familiar cartons of cigarettes. Since the opening of the Horizon Factory with its modern technology, cigarettes can now be manufactured at the rate of 7,000 cigarettes a minute. *(VI)*

An advertising display for Players cigarettes when smoking was almost universal. Players' first trademark was the Nottingham Castle, registered in 1877, but the most famous logo is the familiar sailor's head. *(VI)*

The Players advertising boat which took part in many parades around the country, with Bill Lambton, the driver, on the left. Carnival Queens with their attendants would arrive at showgrounds sitting precariously on the deck of the boat. Owing to an oversight, *Hero*, the boat's name, appears without the letters HMS. When the trademark was registered by Players, the letters were omitted and it was never possible to add them. *(VI)*

Draughtsmen at Raleigh Industries in 1950 when its bicycle factory was the largest in the world. The company has continued to bring out new designs of bicycles, beginning in the 1960s with the RSW 16 – a unisex cycle – followed by the Chopper, beloved of youngsters. *(VI)*

Women checking bicycle parts at Raleigh Industries, 1950. The workforce was then over 7,000, and although the work was monotonous jobs were secure. *(VI)*

Mechanics working on a Raleigh truck, 1950. Besides all types of pedal cycles the firm then also made motorcycles, three-wheel cars and small delivery vans. By the 1980s, as the competition from cheap imports from Far Eastern manufacturers increased, Raleigh began to cut back its production and in 1999 all manufacture ceased. Today all Raleigh bicycles are imported but are still made to the company's high standard of workmanship. *(VI)*

Opposite, top: Assembling bicycles at Raleigh, 1950. Alan Sillitoe in *Saturday Night and Sunday Morning* gives a realistic account of working on a lathe on the shop floor. Bicycles were then being produced at the rate of a million a year and a threat from Far Eastern countries was unimaginable. *(VI)*

Opposite, bottom: Workers load cycles into vans at the Raleigh works, 1950. Raleigh had acquired the Rudge Whitworth Company in 1943, and in 1954 they added the Triumph Company, followed in 1957 by the BSA Cycle Company. *(VI)*

The bookbinding department in the Boots printing works on Station Street, 1953. As well as binding books for customers, the department regularly rebound the books from Boots Book Lovers Libraries. The printing works were rebuilt in 1952, after the old building was destroyed in the blitz on Nottingham in 1941. *(VI)*

Opposite, top: The interior of Boots D.10 building, otherwise known as the Wets Factory, 1955. Designed by Sir Owen Williams and opened in 1933, the factory was immediately hailed as a masterpiece. Time has confirmed that view and it is now a Grade I listed building of outstanding architectural and historical importance. Jesse Boot's dream was to build model factories surrounded by houses similar to those at Bournville and Port Sunlight, but it was his son John who was to fulfil at least part of his vision. *(The Boots Co. PLC)*

Opposite, bottom: Tablet filling in Boots D.6 Factory in the 1950s. The Dry Factory, as it became known, was designed by Sir Owen Williams in 1938, but D.6 never had the same renown as the D.10 Factory. *(The Boots Co. PLC)*

Girls check lisle stockings at
I. & R. Morley's factory in Daybrook,
1950. Morley's were founded in 1799
but it was after Samuel Morley took
control in 1860 that the company
expanded – factories were opened in
Manvers Street, Handel Street, Daybrook
and Heanor. By the twentieth century
Morley's were one of the biggest
employers in the area, but the change in
fashion in the 1960s, from quality fully-
fashioned stockings to tights, brought
about the collapse of the firm. *(VI)*

A lace machine operative (or twisthand)
corrects a fault in the lace on a Leavers
machine at Simon, May & Co., in
Weekday Cross, 1950. Nottingham's
traditional lace industry in the postwar
years was in serious decline, and a
number of local firms were struggling to
survive. *(VI)*

Girls making underwear at David Gibson Ltd, Stoney Street, 1949. The staff were entertained while they worked by music relayed over loudspeakers by Rediffusion. A notice on the wall orders all operatives to leave the workroom during the lunch and tea breaks and to switch off lights as an economy measure. *(VI)*

Women machinists at Meridian on Haydn Road, 1950. This was the time of full employment when firms such as Meridian, Cooper & Roe, Bairnswear and William Hollins had full order books from overseas customers. *(VI)*

Machinery is hoisted into Frymann & Fletcher's knitted fabric business at the Clyde Works, Denison Street, 1949. This difficult operation obviously needed a pair of crane drivers with cool heads. The tenement building was home to a variety of trades, the majority being related to the lace industry. *(VI)*

Barnet's sweet factory in Hartley Road in the late 1940s. The firm was founded in 1898 by Richard Barnet, who began by making sweets in the kitchen of his home in Hyson Green. The company is famous for Barnips cough sweets which it still continues to produce. During the war production continued as rationing of sugar did not apply to cough sweets. *(VI)*

5

Commerce

A Nottingham housewife shopping in an austere shop, 1952. Food rationing was to continue until 1954 but in spite of restrictions people were generally eating a healthy diet. *(VI)*

The Central Market in 1950 when it had become an established feature of the city. The doubts of the stallholders, initially dismayed at moving from the Great Market Place in 1928, were gradually overcome. Steward & Brewill, Wicks and Pettits were among the well-known nurserymen who had stalls down this avenue. *(VI)*

Opposite, top: A hive of activity at the Sneinton Wholesale Market, 1963. Completed in 1938 the market concentrated all the wholesale distributors of fruit, vegetables, flowers, fish and meat. From the early hours of the morning the market resembled a miniature Covent Garden. The market remained in Sneinton until 1995 when it was relocated to Meadow Lane. *(NEP)*

Opposite, bottom: The fish section of the Central Market displaying incredible varieties of fish, 1970. Near the street entrance is the cockle and whelk stall with a group of people enjoying these delicacies. *(JL)*

Women being served at MacFisheries Food Centre on South Parade, 1954. Food rationing had recently ceased and there was more variety in the shops. Smoked haddock was on display at 1s 3d a pound, and mussels were 11d a pound. Frozen fish fingers which had just been introduced by Birds Eye were also on sale. *(VI)*

Jack Ward's fish and chip shop on Carlton Road, 1965. The business was begun in 1899 by his father and was one of seven fish and chip shops which then lined the road between Sneinton Market and Carlton Hill. *(JDW)*

A fresh fish shop in Hyson Green in 1953 when this type of shop was quite common in the suburbs. The price of fish ranged from 1s 6d a pound for kippers to 3s 4d a pound for turbot. Rabbits, which were fairly cheap, were regularly eaten in those days. (FWS)

Joseph Burton's assistants line up behind their fish counter, 1953. Burton's of Smithy Row was at the upper end of the food market and always produced imaginative displays. (VI)

Joseph Burton's magnificent display in the Exchange Arcade for the Coronation of Queen Elizabeth II in 1953. The company began window displays in the 1930s and its effort for the 1937 Coronation of George VI won the first prize in the *Daily Mail* competition. *(VI)*

Joseph Burton's display of replicas of the Crown Jewels and Regalia for the Coronation in 1953. Most Nottingham shops and department stores had patriotic window displays at this time but Burton's eclipsed all the others. *(VI)*

Burton's Christmas decorations in the Exchange Arcade, 1954. The company, along with its rival Skinner & Rook on Long Row, was well known for its high class produce, but at Christmas Burton's drew crowds simply to view their decorations. *(VI)*

The staff of Dawson's butcher's shop, Hyson Green, 1950. This photograph appears to have been taken before Christmas from the number of chickens and turkeys in display in the shop windows. *(VI)*

A coal man in Ewart Street, Forest Fields, in the 1950s – now a diminishing sight. This was the decade when the closure of coalmines began, with more oil-fired power stations being built and householders switching to central heating. *(FWS)*

Darby's glass and china shop in Market Street, 1950. The shop had a reputation for excellence and George Darby who owned it was noted for his old-world courtesy. The business was begun by his mother – Augusta Darby – in 1869 and it moved here in 1884, finally closing in 1954. *(VI)*

Stewart's bulb and seed shop in Market Street, 1953. The shop was opened here in 1889 and after moving to Pelham Street in 1953, Stewart's finally relocated to George Street. The last bulb and seed merchant in the city centre, Stewart's eventually closed in 2002. *(VI)*

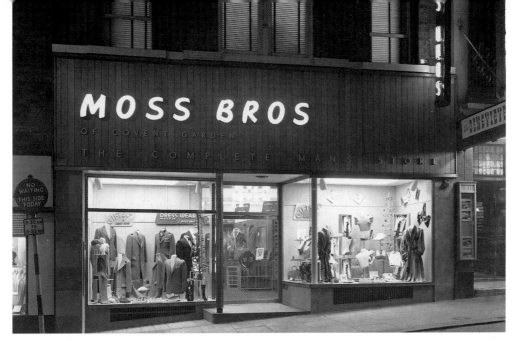

Moss Bros the tailors in Market Street in 1953 in the premises vacated by Stewart's the seedsmen. Moss Bros of Covent Gardens are famous for their hire-wear, particularly of dress clothes. The company eventually moved to the Victoria Centre and have recently opened a shop in Pelham Street. *(VI)*

Boyds, Long Row, in 1954 when the shop was having a promotion with Arthur Askey, who had become a popular TV star, as the attraction. After the 1953 Coronation, a television was an essential item of household equipment and electrical retailers were quick to capitalise on this. TV sets in those days were more cabinet than screen and for most families hire-purchase was the only option. *(VI)*

Star Stores, Lower Parliament Street, decorated for the Coronation in 1953. This small department store, built in the early 1930s, was convenient for shoppers at the nearby Central Market, but after the closure of the market in 1972 its days were numbered. The building is now occupied by Antibo – an Italian restaurant. *(VI)*

The underwear department in Star Stores, 1953. The young boy seems uncomfortable, and his mother appears disapproving of the glamorous nightdresses on display. Their prices vary from £1 5s 6d to £1 6s 5d – perhaps also a shock to her. *(VI)*

Montague Burton's tailors' shop at the corner of Lower Parliament Street and Clumber Street, 1950. The shop was part of a chain of stores which advertised made-to-measure suits for £12 15s, and advised customers to purchase an extra pair of trousers for £2. *(VI)*

Boots Day and Night branch in Wheeler Gate was a Nottingham institution until it closed in 1962. Seen here in 1950 the shop, which opened in 1917, was extended and given a new fascia in 1933. Like all Boots shops of the time, the windows were filled from top to bottom with items for sale – from patent medicines to toiletries and gifts. *(JDW)*

Boots Lister Gate branch in the 1950s, when the company possessed shops in most main streets of the country. Nottingham, the home of Boots, had more branches than any other provincial city. The branch closed in 1962 when this stretch of Lister Gate was redeveloped. (*The Boots Co. PLC*)

Opposite, top: Women at work in the C.B. Laundry, Meadow Lane, 1950. Besides using electric hand irons, the women also employed industrial steam presses. In the 1950s sheets were washed and ironed for 1*s* and blankets for 3*s*. (*VI*)

Opposite, bottom: Cripps' motor car showroom in Lower Parliament Street in the 1950s. The cars are the latest models from the Earls Court motor show, and streamlining is in evidence. A Hillman Minx de luxe saloon car is on sale for £480 and a Sunbeam-Talbot coupé is £845. Motor car showrooms are no longer situated in city centres – this building is now an Argos warehouse. (*VI*)

The typing pool at Strodex in New Basford, 1951. Office workers then had more esteem than factory hands, although their pay was rarely as high. Shorthand-writing and touch-typing are both skills which are becoming increasingly rare. *(VI)*

A telephone switchboard operator at William Hollins' Viyella House on Castle Boulevard, 1950. Incoming telephone calls were transferred to internal phone extensions by plugging cables into a switchboard. *(VI)*

Sub-editors at the *Nottingham Evening Post*, 1961. Their task is highly skilled with one eye on the clock: having received a story they edit and shape it and finally write an arresting headline. Sub-editors can take a poor story and by their editorial ability turn it into an eye-catching piece. *(NEP)*

The *Nottingham Evening Post* print room, 1961. Workers are producing the semi-cylindrical metal plates which are cast from the papier-mâché moulds of each page of the newspaper. The plates are then trimmed and locked onto the printing cylinders of the presses. In between spells of inactivity the printers work at a frantic pace to enable the newspapers to be on the streets within the shortest space of time. *(NEP)*

The eccentric inventor Rowland Emett in the Victoria Shopping Centre, 1973. He was unveiling his latest creation – a 23ft water fountain and clock which on the hour and half-hour becomes a whirling spectacle of birds and butterflies, accompanied by harpsichord music of Purcell. *(LB)*

A pair of Shipstone's horses pulling a dray loaded with barrels of beer on Radford Road, 1968. These splendid animals were a common sight on the city's roads and the brewers continued to use them for publicity purposes when ordinary deliveries were made by Foden motor vehicles. In the background is Heathcote's, a well-known and long-established photographic business. *(JL)*

6

Transport

Payne's excursion train from New Basford to London in 1951. The staff of P.P. Payne Ltd, advertising tape manufacturers, are on their way to the Festival of Britain exhibition on the South Bank of the River Thames. All the major employers of the city hired one or more trains to carry their employees on an annual outing, either to the seaside or to London for sightseeing and a musical show. *(VI)*

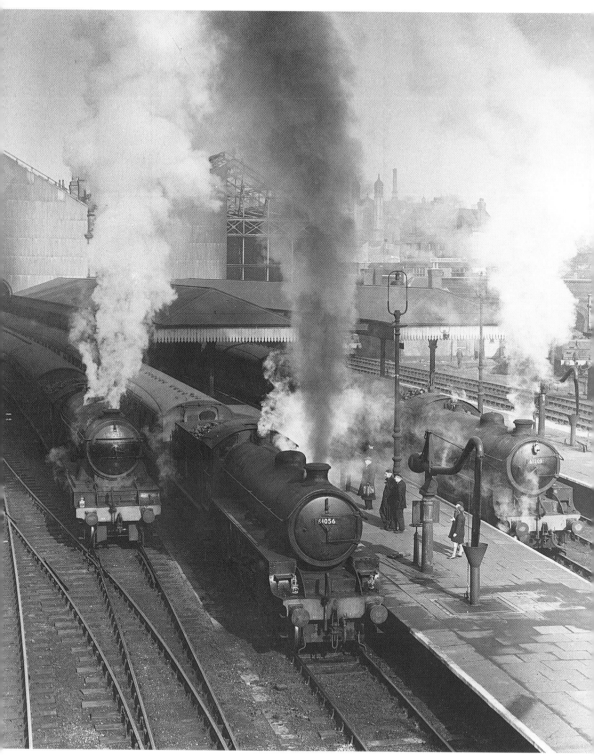

Locomotives billowing smoke and steam into the air at the Victoria Railway Station, 1951. This was a common sight in those days, but today railway enthusiasts would travel miles to view such a scene. They would recognise the locomotive on the left as a class A3 no. 60052 Prince Palatine and the two on the right as class B1s. *(FWS)*

Porters casting shadows on the platform at the Victoria Station, 1951. This photograph captures the atmosphere of a station which is sadly missed. *(FWS)*

The last train to leave from Victoria Station on 2 September 1967. Dr Richard Beeching's recommendation that the Great Central line should be closed, signalled the end of this great station. *(NEP)*

George Chambers, the driver of the last train from the Victoria Station in 1967. This was the 5.34 p.m. diesel train to Rugby, with most of the passengers being rail enthusiasts making a sentimental last journey from the station. Trains continued to run on the line for two more years, departing from Arkwright Street Station – then it, too, was closed. *(NEP)*

Opposite: Wilfred Cook, the porter who was left to run the Victoria Station almost single-handed in the last months of its life in 1967. The photograph shows the almost cathedral-like qualities of the station which the Midland Station does not possess. Within days of its closure the demolition gangs moved in and began dismantling the ironwork – platform seats and signs became collectors' items to be treasured. *(NEP)*

Platform 3 at the Midland Railway Station, 1951. The London train is ready to depart but the platform is beginning to fill up with passengers awaiting the next train. This is in all probability a train bound for the coast judging by the family groups in the foreground. *(NEP)*

Opposite, top: A Fowler 535 locomotive slowly hauling a train through floods at the Midland Station in 1947. These floods – the last major floods in the city – caused widespread disruption in the lower parts of Nottingham. *(FWS)*

Opposite, bottom: The Jubilee class no. 45611 *Hong Kong* locomotive heading a train running through floods at Radford Station in 1947. The overflowing of the River Leen was a regular occurrence in the 1940s. The station on the Midland line was to remain open until 1964. *(NEP)*

A men's outing by Robin Hood coach in 1949. The bus company was founded in 1929 by G.V. Dennis who in that year began a Nottingham to Blackpool service. Robin Hood also had a licence to run tours and excursions – this one being from the Rose and Crown in Northgate, New Basford. In 1961 Barton's acquired Robin Hood's fleet of nineteen coaches and with it the logo of the famous outlaw. *(VI)*

An Armstrong Siddeley coupé in Chapel Bar, 1947. The car, with American styling, is very eye-catching. Across the street is Henry Barker's furniture store – now the Central Library – then with very unusual convex windows. *(JDW)*

Wheeler Gate at night, 1965. The road was then the main route between the Old Market Square and Trent Bridge and was often the scene of traffic jams. *(JDW)*

A traffic hold-up on Upper Parliament Street, 1965. This was caused by the poles of a trolley bus coming off the overhead wires – an occurrence which would cease the following year when these vehicles were removed from service. *(JDW)*

Mount Street Bus Station, 1965. The station was never very successful, always having had the appearance of being temporary. It was built on the site of seventeenth- and eighteenth-century houses and also a Baptist graveyard. In the middle distance are three distinctive buildings, the box-shaped Nottingham Playhouse, with behind it the tower of the Albert Hall and the spire of St Barnabas Cathedral. *(JDW)*

Opposite, top: A bus conductor taking fares on a Nottingham Corporation bus near the bus depot on Manvers Street, 1951. This was the year in which the transport department experimented for a short period with one-man bus operation. Although a rear-entry bus was used, the driver was required to collect fares and then return to his cab to continue the journey. *(VI)*

Opposite, bottom: Queueing for a holiday coach at the Huntingdon Street Bus Station, 1964. Most holidays were spent in Britain at this time, although foreign travel was becoming more popular. Coach travel, although slower than rail, was cheaper and the local coach operators ran services to most coastal resorts. *(NEP)*

A variety of transport in Victoria Street, 1946. The horse patiently pulling the LMS Express Parcels wagon was one of a dwindling number on the city's roads. Behind the no. 3 bus is a trolley bus: these were to remain in service until 1966. The right-hand side of this street was lined with banks and insurance companies. The left-hand side had retail businesses – Armitages the grocers, Robinsons' paint and wallpaper showrooms and Lewis & Grundy, ironmongers – all now closed. *(NEP)*

7

Entertainment & Recreation

Pleasure craft moored by the Plaisaunce Yacht Club, 1951. The crews of these boats are obviously enjoying being on the river without any of the work involved in crewing the craft. *(VI)*

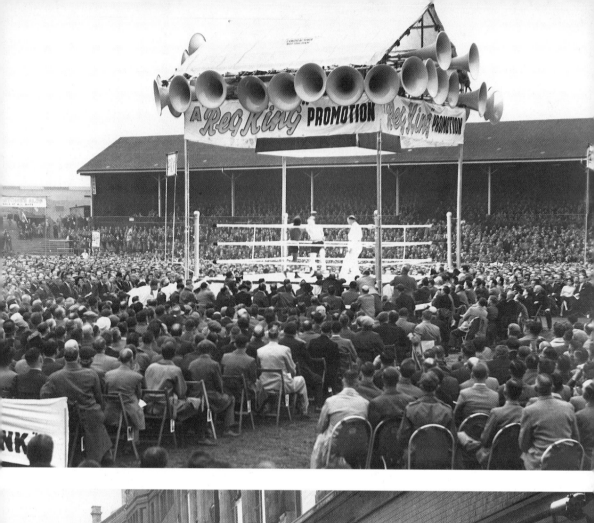

A troupe of acrobats in the Roberts Bros Circus, 1973. The programme at circuses then also included lion taming, horseback riding, knife throwing, illusionists, tumblers and clowns. *(VI)*

Opposite, top: A boxing match at the Notts County football ground, 1952. The fight was promoted by Reg King, a local man who rose from being a milk roundsman to one of the leading fight promoters in the country. This, the main fight of the evening, was between Roy Ankrah, the Empire featherweight champion from the Gold Coast of West Africa and the Frenchman Raymond Famechon, the European champion. The match before a crowd of 30,000 spectators ended in a convincing points victory for Famechon. *(VI)*

Opposite, bottom: Circus elephants trudge down Friar Lane, 1973. These were leading the parade of animals on their way to the Forest where Roberts Bros were presenting their circus. Animal acts with elephants or lions and tigers were then more common, and a parade through the streets before the circus was almost obligatory. *(LB)*

The days of cloth caps at football matches. Notts County in their black and white shirts are playing Chesterfield at Meadow Lane in 1957 – a match which the home team won 2–1. After Tommy Lawton and Jackie Sewell left the club in the early 1950s Notts County went into decline and the record attendances of those days were never to be repeated. *(VI)*

The Nottinghamshire County Cricket team, 1953. Standing, left to right: K. Smales, R.G. Giles, J.D. Clay, B. Dooland, E.J. Martin, F.W. Stocks, E.A. Meads, G. Goonesena. Seated: A. Jepson, H.J. Butler, R.T. Simpson (captain), J. Hardstaff, C.J. Poole. Nottinghamshire had just been joined by two overseas players, Bruce Dooland and Gamini Goonesena, who made an immediate improvement to the fortunes of the team. *(VI)*

Staff at the Nottingham Ice Stadium resurfacing the ice, 1950. After a skating session or ice-hockey match, the ice would be skimmed and re-iced before the next session. The stadium was built in 1939 and was requisitioned by the Air Ministry for the duration of the war. In 1946 the Nottingham Panthers ice-hockey team was formed and immediately attracted enthusiastic crowds to their matches. *(FWS)*

A tussle on the ice between Eddy Plata (Nottingham Panthers) and Gerry Corriveau (Paisley Pirates) as they race along the boards in an ice-hockey match at the Ice Stadium in 1958. *(NEP)*

Goose Fair from Gregory Boulevard, 1950s. The new sensation of the fair is the Diving Vampire Jets, which appear very realistic. The old favourites are all here – the helter-skelter, swingboats, cakewalk, dodgems and the horses. There was still an avenue of side shows including Ron Taylor's boxing booth, a Wild West show, a flea circus and a mouse town. Candyfloss was on sale as well as hot dogs and the great Goose Fair favourites, Grantham gingerbread and brandy-snap. *(FWS)*

Opposite: The Moon Rocket at the Goose Fair in 1960, with two youths apparently the only possible customers. The afternoon sunshine creates a picture of tranquillity – later the roundabout will spin ever faster, the lights will flicker on and off and the music will blare even louder. *(FWS)*

Boys play on the frozen Grantham Canal in 1947. There was no need to use the Lady Bay Bridge or the Swing Bridge to cross the canal in that ferociously cold winter – the water was frozen solid for several weeks. *(JDW)*

Opposite, top: Boys are fishing for minnows in the River Leen in Old Basford, 1954. This harmless pastime gave children endless fun – although the fish never seemed to live beyond a day or two in a jam jar. *(FWS)*

Opposite, bottom: Children play in the shallow River Leen in Old Basford, 1954. It is a warm summer's afternoon with the youngsters either playing at the water's edge or better still, paddling in the stream. *(FWS)*

Highfields Lido, 1947. After the worst winter of the century the weather relented and Britain was treated to a long hot summer, although from the few swimmers in the pool it appears the water here may not have been too warm. *(JDW)*

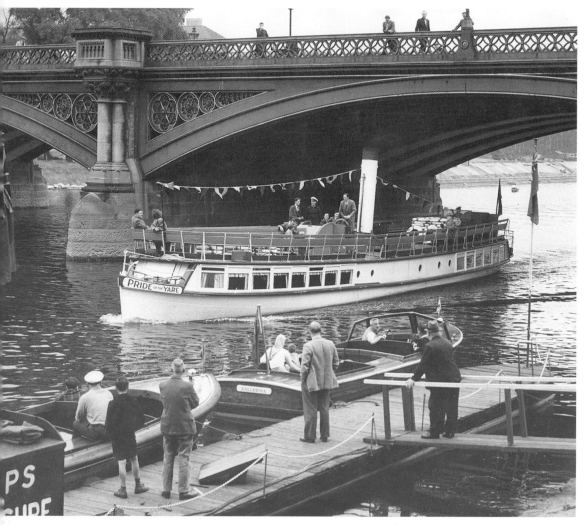

The *Pride of the Yare* passes Turney's Quay, 1951. This pleasure boat which plied between Trent Bridge and Colwick was one of the 'little ships' which ferried troops back from Dunkirk in 1940. The motor launch *Ballerina* moored at the pontoon was regularly employed by the Revd Arthur H. Bird of the Bridgeway Hall to give riverside services. *(FWS)*

Opposite: Languid sunbathers on river craft moored at the Plaisaunce Yacht Club, 1951. Boating was returning to normal after the end of petrol rationing in 1950, although these boats seem to be permanently tied to the pontoons. In the distance are the intrusive chimneys of the North Wilford Power Station. The station was opened in 1925 and continued producing electricity for the Nottingham area until it closed in 1981. *(VI)*

The Plaisaunce Yacht Club, 1951. This was built in 1897 as a summer house for Jesse Boot – somewhere he could retreat to at weekends. Not only was it large enough for his family, but it contained a dance hall and tearooms. In the extensive gardens, tennis courts and sports grounds were laid out for the use of Boots employees. During the summer months entertainments, tea parties and swimming galas were held – with fireworks in the late evening. After Jesse Boot's virtual retirement to Jersey in 1920 the Plaisaunce became the Boots Sports Club. In 1932 the house was sold for £1,900 and was then opened as the Plaisaunce Yacht Club. *(VI)*

The Plaisaunce Yacht Club and next to it, Ivydene, built in 1910. This house still remains, and is now occupied by J.H. Trease, chartered accountants, but the Plaisaunce was pulled down in 1961 when the Rivermead flats were built. *(VI)*

The rowing boat attendant at Colwick Park, 1950. Trips to Colwick by pleasure boat were still popular although the entertainments were not the draw they had been during the pre-war years. Colwick Hall, then owned by the Home Brewery Co., is on a quiet backwater of the river where both boating and fishing could be enjoyed. *(FWS)*

Opposite: Rowing boats being towed on the Nottingham Canal near Carrington Street, 1950. These are Thomas Trevithick's boats on their way to the River Trent from his boatyard at Gregory Street, Lenton. In the early postwar years Trevithick's and Thomas Brookhouse both hired out small boats on the River Trent as well as running motor launches. *(FWS)*

The Royal Canadian Air Force Pipe Band at Wollaton Park, 1953. A military tattoo to commemorate the Coronation of Queen Elizabeth II was held here with the armed services of the United Kingdom and the Commonwealth taking part. Each evening of the tattoo the formal gardens were floodlit and tableaux of famous historic events were presented. *(NEP)*

A multi-talented street musician in a back street of Nottingham, 1950s. Today's buskers are more likely to have an amplifier with them to enhance their music. *(FWS)*

Opposite, top: The Nottingham Junior Harmonic Orchestra with their conductor, Percival Leeds, at the Albert Hall in 1955. The orchestra was formed in 1941 and was composed of local schoolchildren with an average age of fourteen or fifteen, although their repertoire was no different from any other orchestra. *(VI)*

Opposite, bottom: Basil Halliday's band in the Elizabethan Rooms, Upper Parliament Street, in 1953. Basil Halliday formed his first orchestra in 1938 and regularly performed at the Mayfair Ballroom in Long Eaton. In 1949 his band, then known as the Basil Halliday Broadcasting Band, played on the floating bandstand on the River Trent during the Quincentenary celebrations. *(VI)*

A family enjoying the sunshine in the Memorial Gardens on the Victoria Embankment in the 1950s. The gardens were the gift of Jesse Boot who made the announcement of his offer in his acceptance speech when he received the Freedom of the City of Nottingham in 1920. *(FWS)*

Opposite, top: The Palais de Danse, 1969. This, the most famous dance hall in the city, was opened in 1925 on the site of the House of Correction. The building was designed in the Egyptian style which was very popular at the time, with the recent discovery of Tutankhamun's tomb. Besides having a globe above the entrance which flashed red, white and blue colours, the hall boasted an 18ft fountain in the centre of the dance floor. After a spell as Ritzy's and again as the Palais the hall has now been completely refurbished as Oceana – a multi-purpose entertainment venue. *(JL)*

Opposite, bottom: Teddy boys and girls at the Cocked Hat, Broxtowe Lane, 1956. This was the decade when youths wore drape suits, drainpipe trousers and crêpe-soled shoes – their hair, with a huge quiff, would be heavily brylcreemed. Their girl partners favoured circular skirts with their hair in a pony tail. *(LB)*

The May Queens and their attendants at a May Day parade on the Forest, 1950s. The parade, which was organised by the local trade unions, travelled from the Old Market Square and ended on the Forest where the judging of the decorated floats took place. *(FWS)*

Young boys in their home-made hats enjoying party food at a Coronation celebration at St Christopher's church hall in 1953. *(SW)*

8

St Ann's & Sneinton

Princess Terrace, leading from Shelton Street to Northumberland Street, in 1968, with the Princess Royal public house at the bottom of the street on the left. The redevelopment of St Ann's was under consideration from the early 1960s and although the first estimate of houses to be demolished was 3,000, the final figure was 10,000 out of a total of 11,500. *(AA)*

The junction of Lower Parliament Street and Huntingdon Street, with the Post Office sorting office on the right, 1960. In the middle distance is the Huntingdon Street Bus Station which was to remain for a further twelve years. The two white buildings to the right are the Locarno Bingo, previously the Victoria Ballroom and the New Empress Cinema, which was shortly to close. In the distance are the tightly packed terrace houses of St Ann's. *(NEP)*

The Post Office sorting office, Huntingdon Street, 1955. Built in 1938, during the Second World War it was the main Forces Post Office and all mail to and from the armed services was dealt with here. With the opening of the ultra-modern sorting office at Beeston this office closed. The building has now had ten extra storeys added to become an apartment block. *(FWS)*

The Mecca Bingo, St Ann's Well Road, 1973. Also known as the Empress Social Club this was, until 1960, the New Empress Cinema – the decade when many local cinemas were either converted to bingo halls or were closed down. The Empress was demolished during the clearance of St Ann's to make way for a car park. *(AA)*

Westminster Bank, Commercial Square, in 1970, when the building was already scheduled for demolition. The bank, originally the Nottingham & Notts Bank, was designed by Watson Fothergill in 1900. Despite objections to its destruction, this typical Fothergill building was pulled down. The Oliver Cromwell public house on the right-hand corner suffered the same fate as the bank, one of the forty-five pubs of St Ann's which were demolished in the 1970s. *(AA)*

Woodborough Road Baptist Church in 1973, with a happy message on the outside wall. The church was built in 1894 by Watson Fothergill and was one of the few public buildings to survive the clearance of St Ann's. It is now the Pakistan Centre. *(AA)*

St Michael's Police Lodge or Lammas Lodge, as it was known locally, 1968. Built in 1860, this was a police house with a drinking fountain attached and situated in St Michael's Recreation Ground, Millstone Lane – subsequently Huntingdon Street. When the lodge was demolished in 1975 the bells and borough arms from the building were taken to the Brewhouse Yard Museum. *(AA)*

Gladys Spink's beer-off at the corner of Gordon Road and Simkin Street, 1950. This was a proverbial corner shop, appearing to sell most items of food besides having a beer licence. After the redevelopment of St Ann's new shops were built in precincts but the residents of the area never had the same affection for them as they had for the old shops. *(VI)*

Members of the Nottingham Fire Brigade give advice on the prevention of fire to householders in Hutchinson Street, 1965. This was part of a national campaign to spread awareness of fire risks. *(JDW)*

Children at the corner of Union Road and Northumberland Street, 1970. These youngsters from St Ann's appear happy at the demolition of their old houses and the chance to find something of value in the debris. *(AA)*

Sewer pipes on the wasteland of St Ann's, 1970. The houses on St Ann's Well Road still stand, as well as Ashforth's factory on the skyline, but all were to disappear in the next few years. *(LB)*

The Rio Cinema, Oakdale Road, 1955. The cinema opened in November 1939 – advertised as the Bakersfield luxury cinema – presenting *Heart of the North*, an instantly forgettable film starring Dick Foran. As with many other cinemas the spread of television affected its audiences, and the Rio closed in 1959. Five years later the cinema was converted into a music hall with Tommy Trinder appearing at its reopening. In 1967 the final curtain came down and the ground floor of the building was converted into a supermarket with a snooker hall on the floor above. *(VI)*

Opposite, top: The Dale Cinema, Sneinton Dale, in 1955 when the Cinemascope film being presented is *Strange Lady in Town*, with Greer Garson. The cinema opened in 1932 showing *Tarzan, the Ape Man*, starring Johnny Weissmuller. *(VI)*

Opposite, bottom: The interior of the Dale Cinema, 1955. The cinema had no balcony and when opened, ticket prices for the lower stalls were 7*d* and 9*d* – the admission prices for the grand stalls were 1*s* and 1*s* 3*d*. The art deco curtains were made by Griffin & Spalding who, besides having a department store, were theatre and cinema contractors. The cinema closed in 1957 and after being occupied for a number of years by the electrical contractors Wireohms it is now occupied by Aerborn, manufacturers of equine equipment. *(VI)*

Regent Hill, off Carlton Road, 1950. This small area of Sneinton Elements was scheduled for demolition, to be replaced by council houses and renamed the Chedworth Estate. *(VI)*

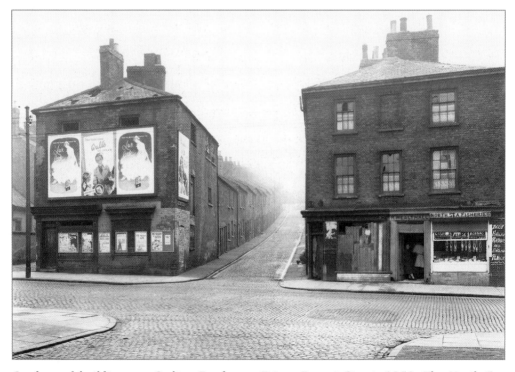

Condemned buildings on Carlton Road near Prince Regent Street, 1950. The North Sea Fisheries on the right were still open, with a row of rabbits – then a staple part of the diet of many people – hanging in the window. *(VI)*

9

Broad Marsh to the River Trent

The junction of Lister Gate, Broad Marsh and Carrington Street, known as 'Lucky Corner', 1964. Montague Burton's art nouveau building is sporting a new fascia and logo. When the building was demolished before the construction of the Broad Marsh Centre the nine carved heads of notable Britons were removed from the façade and attached to a pillar at the bottom of Garners Hill. The building on the left still remains bearing the sign Broad Marsh – probably the shortest street in Nottingham. *(NEP)*

Broad Marsh Bus Station and car park, 1960. Although these have the appearance of being temporary, the area was not to be developed until later in the decade. The houses on the left were then demolished and the construction of the Broad Marsh Centre began. *(JL)*

The Sherwood Rooms, 1970. The dance hall opened in 1938 as the Greyfriars Hall and after being requisitioned by the War Department during the Second World War, it reopened as the Astoria Ballroom. After becoming the Sherwood Rooms in 1957 and later MGM, the hall is now named Ocean but is scheduled for demolition when the Broad Marsh Centre is rebuilt. The building beyond, on Carrington Street, is the electricity showrooms, which was previously the James' store. *(AA)*

The construction of traffic islands at the junction of London Road and Canal Street in 1966 entailed the destruction of the YMCA hostel at this corner. In the middle of the photograph is St Patrick's Church and School, both of which were eventually to be demolished. *(JL)*

St Patrick's Church in Plumptre Square in 1971, when its congregation was already diminishing. In 1979 the church was pulled down and a new church of the same name was built in the Meadows. The Town Arms public house beyond was seriously damaged by fire in the 1980s and subsequently demolished. *(AA)*

A troop of the Royal Army Service Corps leaving the Low Level Railway Station in Great Northern Close in 1952. They were to give mounted displays at the Bath and West Show being held at Wollaton Park. The officers are wearing black armbands in mourning for King George VI. In the background are the Corporation Eastcroft gas works, one of three such plants in the city at this time. *(NEP)*

Opposite, top: The Bridgeway Hall, Arkwright Street in 1964 – a hundred years after it was opened as the Arkwright Street Wesleyan Chapel. In 1925 the Methodist Home Mission made major structural alterations to turn the building into the social centre for the district. Church services, concerts, film shows and talks took place in the hall, which closed in 1965. *(JDW)*

Opposite, bottom: Arkwright Street in 1973, then still lined with small intriguing shops. The demolition of most of the buildings in the street was already scheduled, leaving only a truncated Arkwright Street. In this stretch of the street are two men's tailors, Philip Arnold and Butler Morris, at a time when men almost invariably wore suits. *(LB)*

A stretch of Arkwright Street in 1973 when it was still a thriving thoroughfare. The Meadows service station in the middle distance displays a sign for petrol at 33p a gallon plus quadruple Green Shield stamps. Another poster advertises the forthcoming Second Division football match between the newly promoted Notts County and Sunderland, relegated from the First Division for the first time in their history. *(LB)*

Opposite, top: A row of unusual buildings in Arkwright Street, 1973. Baldwin House on the left, with the mock-Tudor frontage, was the head office of H.J. Baldwin & Co., the company that employed Tommy Lawton as a representative during his playing days at Notts County. Although the shops beyond are unprepossessing, their gabled upper floors are very distinctive. *(LB)*

Opposite, bottom: The Boots Institute and shop at Trent Bridge, 1973. The Tudor style premises were built in about 1907 as a chemist's shop and the Old English Café. The café remained until 1922 when Boots opened their social club here, providing a billiard room, lounge, café and dance hall. The shop closed in 1969 and although the social club remains it is now a private club known as the Embankment. *(LB)*

The Globe Picture House in 1955, standing prominently between Arkwright Street and London Road. The film being shown is *Special Delivery* starring Joseph Cotton and Eva Bartok. The cinema opened in 1912 and after flirting with bingo for a short while in 1961 finally closed the following year. *(VI)*

Workmen are catching fish while cleaning the ornamental pond in the Victoria Embankment Memorial Gardens, 1964. The gardens were laid out in 1927 on land given by Jesse Boot for use as a memorial park. The Memorial Arch in the background was designed by T. Wallis Gordon and was unveiled in November 1927. *(NEP)*

Preparing to launch the *Evening News* boat into the floods of the Meadows in 1947. After the heavy snowfalls of the previous winter a sudden thaw in March brought record-breaking floods to the lower parts of Nottingham. The children are enjoying this unusual spectacle. *(NEP)*

An army 'Duck' transporting residents along Briar Street during the floods of 1947. Some families were marooned on the upper floors of their houses for a number of days until the waters subsided. *(NEP)*

Flood defence works in progress near the Suspension Bridge, 1950. After the disastrous floods of 1947 the Trent River Board began widening the river along this stretch and also building concrete barriers. *(VI)*

The swollen River Trent near the Clifton Colliery, 1951. The flood defence works of the previous years although tested were never to be breached. Clifton Colliery, opened in 1870, and the first pit in Britain to be nationalised in 1943, was to close in 1970. *(VI)*

10

The Suburbs

Cottages on Arkers Row, Old Basford, 1965. These small dwellings were built in the nineteenth century for the workers in the lace and hosiery trade and their families. On the outside wall of the centre house hangs a tin bath, as the houses had no bathrooms as well as having no indoor toilets. By the 1960s the city council had plans to demolish the buildings in this area to construct tower blocks to house their residents. *(D. Amos)*

Arkers Row, Old Basford, with some of the houses already shuttered and awaiting demolition, 1965. The new blocks of flats which were built in the district were not destined to survive as long as these cottages. Poor construction and social problems encountered by the tenants led to their being pulled down within fifteen years of their erection. *(D. Amos)*

A shuttered building on Lincoln Street, Old Basford, 1965. This was Rose Bros' old-established grocery shop, and beyond, a steamroller is flattening the site of the Bleachers Arms. This pub was a reminder of the days in the nineteenth century when there were seven bleaching works in the area. *(D. Amos)*

Cecil Howitt council houses on Arnold Road, Bestwood, 1950s. After the city extended its boundary in 1933 to include Bestwood, an estate of council houses was built here, being completed in 1939. The mother and daughter in matching coats have the road to themselves. Also noticeable is the almost complete absence of vehicles. One car can be seen in the distance; also visible is a pile of recently delivered coal on the pavement. *(FWS)*

Commercial Road, Bulwell, 1951.
Freegar's old-fashioned service
station in the centre appears to be
in the process of being rebuilt. The
Mason's Arms on the right, known
to its regulars as Mad Jacks, has
the masonic sign on its front.
These buildings were all pulled
down when the area was
redeveloped. *(VI)*

Old Peveril or Debtors' Prison,
St Peters Street, 1955. This was
originally the Radford Workhouse
which closed in 1838. The Peveril
Prison which had previously been
situated behind the White Hart at
Lenton was transferred here in
1842. After the closure of the
prison in 1849, the building was
converted into two houses which
remained here until 1968. *(JL)*

Radford Lock on the Nottingham Canal, 1947. The canal was closed to traffic in 1936 and was later filled in. The council houses in the distance are on Radford Bridge Road. *(CH)*

A sunny path in Radford, 1950s. This is New Road leading to Hartley Road before the area was developed. On the right is the Midland Railway just north of Radford Station. *(FWS)*

Alfreton Road, when it was a shoppers' paradise, 1951. Marsdens the grocers, in the centre, was a company with numerous branches – it was closed in the 1960s. Behind the two motor cars are the premises of Victor Cresswell, a wholesale hosier whose business expanded to become Victor Fashions in Traffic Street. *(VI)*

Old and new dwellings in Radford, 1964. These are the almost completed flats off Hartley Road, viewed from Edinburgh Street. The terraced houses were shortly to be demolished and replaced by modern housing. *(JDW)*

The TIL house in Clifton in the 1950s. This is named after Thomas Lambert, who in 1707 refaced the original wattle and daub cottage and added a wing to the house. A Nottingham couple who bought the house in 1994, when it was in a dilapidated state, have now restored the building to its former glory. *(FWS)*

Opposite, top: Children collect the groceries by sledge in the snow at Wollaton, 1947. These youngsters are having fun while performing an everyday chore. *(JDW)*

Opposite, bottom: German prisoners-of-war are helping to clear a road at Wollaton, 1947. The men are from the nearby camp in Wollaton Park and in that severe winter were a great help in keeping the minor roads clear. *(JDW)*

ACKNOWLEDGEMENTS

I particularly wish to thank John Watson of Viva Imaging (*VI*) for allowing me access to their huge collection of glass plates inherited from Marshall & Co. – one of Nottingham's foremost commercial photographers. I should also like to thank the following for the loan of photographs: David Amos, David Archer, Alan Atkinson (*AA*), The Boots Co. PLC, Leonard Brownlow (*LB*), Clive Hardy (*CH*), John Lock (*JL*), John (Jack) Middleton (*JM*), Nottingham City Council Leisure and Community Services – Local Studies Library (*LSL*), *Nottingham Evening Post* (*NEP*) and Stephen Williamson (*SW*). The photographs of F.W. Stevenson (*FWS*) are reproduced by permission of Mrs May Sentance.

Once again I wish to thank Dorothy Ritchie and the staff of the Local Studies Library for their kindness and help, and also the following for their assistance: Terry Buck, Elena Botterill, Anita Logue, David Slater, Jane Tomkinson, Alan Trease and Rick Wilde.

My special thanks, as always, to my wife Margaret for her continued help and advice.

Nottingham-by-the-Sea, 1950. The bracing air at Skegness has drawn Nottingham families for decades and those loyal to the resort return year after year. (*FWS*)